Living in My Place
With Me

Living in My Place
With Me

The Mask Has Been Removed

ANGELA SWEETENBERG

Living in my Place with Me

Published by:
Professional Woman Publishing
www.pwnbooks.com

ISBN: 978-0-9987636-0-6

Introduction

In life, I have found that the power of love is so great! The power that I hold within is life changing; I have been able to change my life by changing my thoughts and my responses. Learning to love myself has been the key to it all. This alone has helped me understand the connection between myself and others. For years, I was unable to fully engage in relationships with other people because I didn't truly love myself. Of course, I didn't recognize what was happening until much later in life but when I did, things started to shift.

I never understood why I was not completely happy or why I would only go so far, why I would push to be great at work, but not in my personal life. I made life-altering decisions and left a job after ten years to pursue something that was truly not right for me. This was the result of fear and insecurity. I put on a mask and looked great on the outside but inside I was all torn up.

My transformation started in 2002 when my marriage failed. I came home and realized that I needed to completely start over. I needed to know who I was; I mean really know me! I started to write and write and write. For awhile, I could not stop writing. I wrote for myself, I wrote for my daughter, I wrote for others. But as I reflect back upon what I wrote, I realize that most of what I had written was speaking directly to me; it was rebuilding and shaping me into who I am today.

I am so grateful for the challenges and the path that I walked to get to this point. It was tough, probably the toughest thing that I have ever had to endure, because I had to look right into the mirror and face me! I needed to know why I was so insecure, why I allowed junk in my life, and why I didn't esteem myself worthy of all the great things that life had to offer. I couldn't even see the gifts and talents that I had, so I could not use them to their fullest. I was limiting myself and didn't even know it. Once I figured out who I was and who I was meant to be, everything started to change. I became a better mother, a better friend, and a better person as a whole. I started to look at things so differently and approach life with a new set of eyes and intent.

My life is meaningful now and taking on new shape every day. This is a continual journey as it should be. As life happens, I have to be able to maneuver, or dance as I call it. One of the things I love to say and you will see this throughout the book, is find the music that makes your heart, soul, mind and body dance. Play it, put it on repeat and DANCE. Instead of bowing down to hurt, pain, relationship failures, unsuccessful ventures and any other challenges, learn to make the best of them and dance through the process.

My transformation shows up in my relationships and interactions with other people; **the mask has been removed.** I am not afraid to showcase who I am because although I am not perfect by any means, I am confident that I can change my life by the way that I choose to live and respond to it. I am not discouraged or afraid of life anymore; I love it and I love the outcome of pushing through and overcoming my fears.

I am especially grateful for my biological and church family, and my friends who have been a great support system. I don't know if I could have done this alone. I want to call out my daughter, Briona.

She has become quite inspirational and I am so proud of her and all of her achievements. As parents, we don't realize the impact that we have on our children until we start to see ourselves in them. At one time, I saw some things that I didn't want to see as it reminded me of myself, but now I love what I see in her. I have now started a move to inspire as many people as I can, specifically women and girls, because I see a great need there.

I am really excited about this chapter in my life and want to share some of my writings in hopes that you will find inspiration, a little laughter or maybe just a good read. You may even find something to share with someone else. Enjoy!

Why Judge? Just Love

You know, it is so hard to see ourselves as beautiful when society lays it out so plainly and on every canvas it looks pretty much the same. When we look into the mirror at ourselves, what we see is that outer shell with blemishes; we don't see what others deem beautiful. We start to internalize external expectations of ourselves and we get discouraged.

As adults, we may or may not have learned to embrace our authentic selves; it's hard and some of us are still struggling. Think about our youth; they tussle with the feeling that they need to fit in. They are not ok with who they are, how they look and can't possibly see their true worth. Confidence and self-esteem are very low which leads to poor decision making, depression and the inability to set goals worthy of their potential.

It took me years! I struggled and made a lot of choices that I probably would not have made otherwise because I didn't believe in myself. I want you to tackle it now. I have learned to look within and really appreciate who I am and when I finally got to know me, I started to see just how beautiful I am from the core and I began to realize my potential and all that I have to offer.

Beauty comes in so many hues and instead of appreciating all of the variety that we offer individually, we have chosen to value and judge based on a very limited, discriminatory view. My agenda is to push women and girls to see and define beauty in themselves and others differently, to CHARM (Change Hearts as a Role Model). Learn to love yourself just the way you are; love all of you! Appreciate all that you are and have to offer and see yourself as a gift. Only then, are you able to drop the bias and judgment and truly see and appreciate others.

I have written a few inspirational pieces that I hope you will enjoy. Being different is normal; we are all created as individuals with very different looks, feelings, special markings and characteristics that were designed just for us. So, refuse to judge, just love!

Different

I am different, not like the rest
I have my own destiny
It serves me best

I didn't just happen
I was a plan
I will not grow like any other can

I will be different
I love that about me
I am an individual, you see

Recognize me
Understand that my place was meant for me
Not him, not her, just me

This is why I can't just be
I have to search and find my key
Then I can live in my place with me

You have a place too
A place designed especially for you
Be proud to be different
There's no one in the world that can be like you
You're an individual too!

Search and find your key
Live boldly in your place
Say to yourself, "I Love Me"

Internal Makeover

I gave myself an internal makeover
All the pain, struggle and grief is over
I looked deep inside to find me
I searched high and low
I found an abundance of strength, an overflow
I tapped into my source of power
I released the pride and donned humility
The very foundation from which I was built
My origination is what freed me from guilt
That same institution of love cradles my peace
I have accepted wisdom
I've dressed myself in new found insight
Purity runs through my veins
My heart pumps truth and love – no more hate, deceit or shame
No more defeat
Triumphant is my new name
Confidence in my strong tower
Every obstacle shall be devoured
I no longer desire to be needy
I've agreed to a new treaty
I am brand new
Now it's time for you to work on you!

Approved

Too dark or too light
Is it my skin tone?
That renders me alright

Too thick or too thin
Is it my size?
That allows me to fit in

So unfair of a man
To measure my worth
Simply by my outer girth

So shallow a mind that
Judges another by mere sight

Afraid to burrow deeper
Afraid his own insecurities
May perhaps, be brought to light

Judge me not
I presume you forgot

I'm another of his creations
He who rules the nations

Your opinion is of no issue
It's of no concern

I'm official and accepted
I've already been approved
The funny thing is, so have you!

No Shame

I am Different and that's ok
I was created this way

There's no shame
No one to blame

There's nothing wrong with me
There would be if I were the same

You can call me whatever
It doesn't matter
Not now, or ever

You can even call me strange
It still won't cause me to change

I have a life that I love living
As I continue to love me
I can just keep on giving

Giving to others who are in desperate need
Giving friendship to those who surround me

Being different says a lot about me
It's who I am
It's what I am
And what I'll always be
It's just me

So, I will say it again and again and again
I'm different and it's ok

I happen to love being this way!

When I Love Myself

When I love myself
I respect myself
I demand the respect of others
I respect others
When I love myself
I take care of me
I keep my mind pure
I keep my words positive
When I love myself
I pray for my friends
I keep the less fortunate close at heart
When I love myself
I humble myself
I love my neighbor
I make peace
I keep peace
When I love myself
I do what I know is right
I speak what I know is true
I judge not another
When I love myself
When I truly love myself
I see myself

I see my weaknesses
I see my strengths
I see criticism as a means of growth
When I love myself
I am a role model
I am a mentor
I am an advocate for self-improvement
When I love myself
I am destined for great things
I know that I was created for a purpose
I work towards achieving my full potential
When I love myself
It shows on the outside
I can help the next man
I have something worthwhile to offer
When I love myself
I have peace
I am happy
I am free!!!

Beauty

The clothes I wear
The way I style my hair
The shoes on my feet
None of this makes me!

Beauty is not just what you see
It's what I hold inside of me

The peace that I keep
The love that flows so deep
The warmth in my heart, even when I sleep

Beauty is never just what you see
It's not the size of my clothes
The width or length of my nose
Nor the space between my teeth

This doesn't even compare to me
How could it possibly make me?

It's what's underneath
It's what I hold inside of me
It's that do all and be all
Of what makes me Me!

It's that joy inside
That makes me kind
Beauty is not always what's on one's mind

Beauty can't be taught
It can't be bought

That inner peace
That willingness to be
It's from whence I speak that makes me unique
That spirit of love flowing out of me
This beauty is what makes me Me!

Mirror

When I look in the mirror, I see Me
I see a perfect creation
Full of Love, Joy and Peace

I see innocent imagination
A pure creation

Strength, Power and Wisdom, it's all inside of me
When I look in the mirror, this too I can see

I am never more proud than when I see me
I look in the mirror and love what I see

I am so proud of my reflection – my mirror gets no rejection!

Learning to Love,
That's All You need!

Dark, Light
Brown, White
No matter my shade
I am beautiful in my sight

Too black
Too pale
I've never seen it measured on a scale

Skin color
It's just a shade
My beauty can never be captured this way

So what if I'm dark
I wasn't meant to be light
No matter what color I am
I can guarantee, I was mixed just right

You say the outside is real light
Believe me, it's not too faint
I look good without the paint

The essence of me rises from deep within
Way beneath my skin
Within my bones
Or even deeper
How deep, no one knows

A shallow mind could never see me
A shallow view will remain confused
Opening your eyes doesn't give you access
Opening your mind, doesn't pass the test

Learning to love, that's all you need
Forgiving and loving you will show you how to love and see me!

Destiny

Not who you want me to be
But who I was created to be

Not what you want for me
But what's already in store for me

Not what you think of me
But what I think of myself

It's not your plan
But the one dealt to my hand

What I choose to do
Let me see it through

For if I make a mistake
The lesson learned is for me

Not You

Smile

Smile always
Even on cloudy days
It doesn't have to rain

Keep your head up
Simply because you've decided not to give up

Smiles can heal hurt if they are real
Smiles can also hide tears and fears
A beautiful smile is often remembered for years and years

You may never know how your smile alone has helped another
How it has eased a mind of worry or trouble

There's something about a smile that's alive
One that's full of energy and drive
There's something about your precious smile
That makes it all worth while

Your smile is contagious
Pass it on
Others crave such a treasure

Never lose that beautiful smile
It just renders another compliment to a Wonderful Child!

Are They a Reflection of You?

Whether we like it or not, our children mirror us, whomever is raising them or someone else who is around as an influence. Make sure that when you are telling your children how proud you are of them, you can credit yourself for passing on some good stuff, not wondering where they got it!

It is so important to be the example; your child's first role model should be you! Mirror the image that you want them to portray. Be proud of your reflection and be your own best friend. They see and feel it when we are not confident and most times they start to take on those same tendencies. Every now and then, we see a child that beats those odds and finds their confidence and strength even though they grew up in an environment thick with insecurity and maybe even negativity.

Now, sometimes our kids are ashamed of us because we are just not what they call cool or we do things that are not quite up-to-date with the young generation. We are parents and we don't fit in all the time and that's ok too. What I am referring to is when our own behaviors contradict what we are teaching and trying to instill in them. This most often, does not work.

Vow to Me

I am my own best friend
I will have me until the end

I will take good care of me
Be true to myself, as true as I can be

Happiness is mine
I'm willing to invest the time

I will smile, laugh and play
I will find joy every day

This not only do I vow today
I will also encourage you the same way

I am happy with me
As happy as I can be

Reflection

I am special and I love me
I will be all that God said I will be
I am proud, I am strong
I am humble, even when wrong

Look at me and be proud too
For I should be a direct reflection of you
And if I am not
Then surely you have some work to do!

What I Love About You

Your mind is pure
Your heart is true

Your gracious ways
Thoughtful
Kind
Patient
So much more, I can say

You have a generous heart
Honesty flows each time your lips part
Words of wisdom
Words of peace
Sacred vows you always keep

You're a friend beyond your years
In my heart, a special place
I will always keep

I'll keep you close
Close to me

I'll treasure you
Just because you're you
And because you make loving you so easy to do!

Girly

Girl, I really love you
You are bold, beautiful, passionate, and confident
You are you!
Girl, I really love you!

Small and mighty! Think about how powerful this short declaration can be when you say it as you are looking in the mirror and seeing yourself, telling your child or someone else's child, calling up your friend or your sister or maybe just taking a chance and telling someone you don't even know. How often do we take the time to tell folks inside our circle how much we love them just the way they are? I know we can easily find reasons not to express ourselves, maybe, they are not doing things the way we want them to or maybe we had a fight or we just have issues expressing ourselves. We hardly ever or never say it to anyone we don't know and if we do, do we really mean it?

Think about it, I love you because you are you. This is profound. It means, I love you even with all of your stuff, all of your moodiness, your insecurities, your shadiness, your poor decision making. I love you even though you keep making the same mistakes over and over, I still love you! I am declaring that you are bold, beautiful, powerful and confident. Now, just in this paragraph, I want you to go back and insert the word me, I, or my everywhere you see "you or your". How did that make you feel?

Women, we are so powerful, so strong! I liken us to a male peacock, please do not get offended. A peacock's wingspan is quite disproportionate to its small body. I imagine their wings are very heavy yet the peacock carries them with grace and confidence. Have you ever watched one spread its wings? It is simply amazing and a beautiful sight. The male peacock is decorated with colorful radiance in his feathers. A woman's life is adorned as a palette of translucent illumination. She unknowingly at times, bears tremendous weight on her tiny shoulders; the weight of motherhood, the weight of inequality in the workforce, the weight of abuse and conformity and so much more. Like the peacock, she carries it and does so without complaint and without regret; she perseveres with every Bold, Beautiful and Confident step she takes toward owning her Authenticity.

Our capacity is so great, yet we often times see ourselves as less than, or undeserving. What will it take for us to move forward knowing that we are powerful beings? How can we shed the baggage of fear and insecurity? Ladies, we have to shed it, spread our wings and walk in confidence knowing that we will always be growing and building ourselves.

Suspend Judgment, Settle for You

Know who you are
Love you
Be you
Love who you have become
And who you are growing into
Suspend judgment of yourself
Otherwise, you can't of anyone else
Let it go, its already done
Use the past
Let it drive you
And give you a better view
Let it teach you
To win from every loss
To grow at all cost
Be courageous, be victorious, settle for you
You will be amazed at who you truly are
And what you can do

Fear, I love you

You encourage me to push beyond invisible limits
You open my mind to a world of possibility
You stretch me, teach me and propel me

You are extinguishable in my world
You light a fire, I become courageous, you cease to exist

I acknowledge your presence even your great power
I choose only to build anytime you interrupt the hour

You are sent to make me better
To make me bolder
To make me stronger

Fear, I don't fear you
I embrace you
I step into absolute confidence when you show up
I am unstoppable
I don't fear you, I love you!

Loving You, Loving Me

In order to love you, I must love me
I have to love me first so that I can achieve all my worth

Times get hard and seem too tough
Its times like this when I remember that God
will never give me too much

I can and I will make it through
If for no other reason than to encourage you

I love me, this is true
That's the key to me loving you

Today is About Me

I am Bold
I am Beautiful
I am Confident
I am Powerful
I am Fearless
I am Amazing
Today is about Me
Today is about Me
Today is about Me

What a great day it is to be about me!

Take time to affirm who you are each day; it's ok, it's not arrogance. It may feel a little bit uncomfortable at first, but once you truly believe that you are all of these things and so much more, it will be easy, I promise. Create your own affirmation and walk in it; you don't have to say it out in public, it will show through you – your energy will scream all of those amazing things that you are internalizing. Know your worth and understand exactly who you are and who you were created to be! It's even better if you look in the mirror and do it!

Friendship

Supporting, caring for and loving each other is what friendship is all about. Now, those three things encompass a whole lot. When we talk about supporting each other that means giving up time, being happy for them when they are successful, we can't be envious. We have to tell our girlfriends the truth when their clothes are too tight and when they need to brush up on some hygiene. Loving our friends comes at a price! The price of loving despite their individuality which is very different from ours most of the time. Sometimes, so different, we wonder where the heck they came from.

Friendship requires action and acknowledgement. It takes time to build and takes an investment to keep it strong. I have made some good friends in life and have made the mistake of not investing time to grow those bonds, so I have lost some of those friends. Sometimes, we allow life and all of its gifts to consume us in the moment and we neglect our friends. Now, more than ever, I am trying to build friendships and doing my best to nurture my relationships so that I can be a good friend. I can't love, care for and support my friends if I don't know them well enough to know what they need or don't spend enough time to even call them friends. I now make the time.

Over the past two years, I have noticed a huge need when it comes to women and girls. The need for support and encouragement. I see a huge lack of confidence and growing insecurities. They suffer with self-esteem issues and don't find comfort in other women and girls who can inspire them. What they find is others just like them who encourage this same behavior because they are in the same boat. I see women and young girls criticize each other, even the ones they call their friends. I don't hear too many females offering to help each other out. Why judge and criticize? Wouldn't we want someone to encourage us, wouldn't we want someone to help if we were in need? Why don't we do it more ourselves? Don't you agree it's time we learn the true value of friendship?

I remember my daughter experiencing issues with friends when she was a teenager. All teenage girls go through this, I believe. I told her to be a good friend and you will be able to spot a good friend. First, you have to be a good friend. I encouraged honesty and care and to treat your friends with respect. I am really proud today because she has developed friendships that have lasted for years. She is now in graduate school and has had some of the same friends since elementary school.

The next group writings was written for my friends and family; others, were written just because…Enjoy!

Charm

Changing Hearts as Role Models

I love myself and I also love you
I commit to being a support system for you
Encouragement is free – I give it to you

I see you the same as I see me
Confident, bold, powerful, passionate and as beautiful as you can be

I change hearts as a role model
I challenge you to do the same
Commit to supporting other women
Encourage our girls
Only see yourself as the most amazing woman on earth

I love me and I love you
Love yourself and love me back
Dare me to just be me
I dare you to fully embrace you

Alone, I CHARM
Together, We CHARM
Join me and see how we expand and add links
to the chain of confident women across the globe!

I Call You Friend

I don't see your faults; I see purpose in you
I smile at you, you look me up and down
I call you beautiful, you deem me unworthy
I save you a seat, you walk past me
I pray for you, you never even think of me
I acknowledge your presence, I am invisible to you

I often wonder, is she blind?
Why so much hurt?
Why does she dismiss her own worth?
Does she feel it's impossible to love herself?

I love you despite your treatment of me
I pray for you; I want you to know love too
I don't see your fault; I see purpose in you
I only wish you could see it too

Open your eyes, mind and heart
Learn to love yourself
You will be amazed at how others will look to you

Unworthy, So Worthy

I see you but you can't see yourself
I love you but you don't love yourself
I cherish you but you only allow me so much
Your hiding place is so deep

I see you when you don't see yourself
I love you when you can't love yourself
I cherish you even though you only allow a shallow peek
Your hiding place is so deep – It frightens me

I worry that you don't know your worth
Your mind is clouded, your vision blurred
Unworthy painted on your canvass
Your destiny, your life, your imagination for sure

So worthy, so worthy your veins bleed
Worthy, worthy you are indeed
Come out of hiding – it's beautiful here
See yourself, love yourself, and cherish your friends

So worthy from the beginning
Happiness without limit
Take hold of your peace
Own it
It's yours to keep

My Friend

I am grateful to call you my friend
You value yourself as much as you value another
A rock for some, a shoulder for others
A pillar that holds the family together

A kind voice that matches your heart
A warm smile that lights a room
An honest tone that speaks to your character
A sensitivity about you outlines true compassion

I am honored when in your presence
Elated to have made your acquaintance
My friend, you are special
Indeed, you are amazing
A treasure worth the find

My friend
In all you do, remain true to you
You are an angel to many
A jovial, gifted and humbled spirit
A peacemaker worthy of all your due

What? Love?

I want love, I forget about friendship
I get emotional and allow hurt to rip,
at my heart, my head and my love
Is it love at all, what is it? How do I know?
How can I tell if I don't know?
Love is visible and love is within and all around you
It sees you, all of you – your faults too
It responds to you, it engages you and patiently waits
for you to engage too
Love pushes you to be better, inspires you to be you
Love sees you – it truly sees you
Love desires for you to be confident
Never intentionally intimidates, always comforts you
Love knows when you are hurt and tries to heal
Love lets go when it's not meant to be
Love wants you to be happy
Love is strong; it nurtures growth in you
Love is a peacemaker
It compromises without fault, blame or shame
Love shoulders you to carry you through
Love will protect you, not harm you
Love is your friend
It invests the time to be your best friend

Love knows love
Love loves others
Love never isolates you
Love challenges you to be courageous and conquer your fears
Love celebrates you and is proud of your accomplishments
Love does not criticize – love encourages you
It's not always politically correct; remember, it's a journey
Love is growing too
Love does not run at the first sign of trouble
Love is tenacious and stays to conquer every obstacles
Love knows love and knows how to love you
Love will be your guide if you get lost
Love will not leave you; it becomes you
Love is the basis for all that you do
Love is diligent
Love is patient
Love is you, Love is me, Love is meant to be

A note to my Friend,

A friend indeed. Thanks for all the joy you've given me
True friendship is hard to find. And you, my dear, are one of a kind
I have never known one quite like you –
compassionate, loving, honest, just plain true
My friend, I feel I owe you much thanks and appreciation
Because of you and your thoughtfulness, your patient and humble
ways I have been able to progress to a much better situation,
a brighter day!

You deserve the absolute best; you stand out above and beyond
the rest. I treasure you my friend, I treasure you.

They always say we need more love, more peace, more of this and
more of that in the world. In my opinion, all we need is more
people with a heart like yours.

May God's blessings and grace be fully bestowed upon you and all
that involves you. May his love and kindness carry you through.

Love,
Your friend

You and I

As I look at the mountains and the clouds in the sky
I begin to recognize beauty before my eyes
A beauty that cannot be disturbed or tainted
A beauty that's not high maintenance

It's quite remarkable this beauty I see
Similar to our beauty, you and me

I love our way of greeting whenever we meet
Our way of sharing our special treats

I love the way we appreciate one another
The way one speaks kindly of the other

The tears of joy shed when one has succeeded
The hurry and get there when the other is needed

I love the way it feels to be your friend
Your best friend as you contend

The from the heart corrections when I'm wrong
The "I miss you's" when I'm gone

The simple hugs you give for no reason
The gifts given in and out of season

There's just something special about what we share
It's a wonderful feeling knowing we care

Beauty doesn't get any better than this
What we have is better than bliss

Sister and a Friend

Sister and a friend
A special love
A gift that I treasure within

A strong soul
Created in unison with Christ
A unity mold

I love your spirit
Your strength and your faith
I admire your ability to love and admonish hate

Unwavering devotion to family
And commitment to God
A true manifestation of His peace
Instilled in your heart

My sister and my friend
My love for you is profound
Expression in words
Can only tap into its depth

No tongue could utter a more perfect sound
The sound of my thoughts
When I think of the love
That I hold for my sister

And my sister alone

A Heart like Yours

If everyone had a heart like yours
They could all inspire and encourage the way that you do
If they just knew how to love without limits
How to pray for those whose faith is diminished
If everyone had a heart like yours
There would be constant praise
Unimaginable kindness and compassion
There would be a spirit of unity and peace
No more oneness and me
If everyone had the mind of Christ
Or even sought after His likes
Then they could share a heart just like yours
A heart that is pure and wholesome
One that dispenses no hurt or pain
A heart that is full of nothing but sheer joy
Even during the rain

From Mom to You

Here are a few notes that I shared with my daughter along the way. This was another way for me to encourage her and show her how I was feeling in the moment. Some of my other writings to her are sprinkled throughout the book.

We laughed at a lot of these and she found them very inspiring. I want to share so that you can see that however we decide to inspire our kids its ok, we just need to make sure we invest the time in them – they need it and deserve it. Sometimes, I would put a poem in her lunchbox or her book bag. Sometimes, I would frame a writing and hang it in her room. What inspired me to start writing to her was one day she came home from school, she was only in first grade and she looked at me and said, "Mommy, I cried in school today." When I asked why, she said "because I couldn't remember what you looked like" and she started crying again. I chuckled a little and immediately put a picture of me in her book bag. And, from that point on, I made it a point to always let her know that I loved her very much. I hope you enjoy these!

My Child

Just know how much you mean to me
I love you without limits
I scold you because my cares are so deep
I want the best for you
I never mean to stress you
I want you to know love
I want you to feel love
I want to be the one to instill love in your heart
I am your mother
I am where it should start
You make me a conscious mom
Reminding me when I am crossing the line
You render me the best mom
Praising me when I make you smile
You keep me an honest mom
Always wanting to be the best example for you
I am sorry if there is ever a time when my intentions are not clear
Promise to talk to me, so we can clear the air
I promise to listen and always be there
There is nothing more important than you and me
And the love we share

In Trouble

When you were small and got in trouble
You'd always say, "I love you" on the double
It never failed
Like clockwork, "I love you" prevailed

It was so cute to hear those words
You knew you had a chance
As soon as it was heard

What a way to turn the tide
"I love you" was always on your side
Sometimes you still got in trouble
Even with the I love you
I had to burst your bubble
If I hadn't you wouldn't have learned
And wouldn't appreciate all those special privileges
you now have earned

So keep the "I love you's" coming my way
There's no telling how it might influence me today!

Teen times

There might come a time when you don't like me so much
That would probably be during that teenage rut
Never fear, that will end too
And believe me, not a moment too soon!

Moods, moods, moods
And then the blues
Oh, how I can never forget those blues
Thank God, I've been there
Now, I know that one day you will be standing in my shoes

Surely, you can weather the storm
And a storm it will be
Just remember, it's not just you
It used to be me!
Right now, it's just your time
And as time passes, you'll be just fine!

I love you,
Mom

Simple Hug

You gave me a hug
It brightened my day
"You're the best mom," you say

Your smile gives me more than just a thrill
It empowers me with an undying will
A will to succeed in raising you
To be the best in everything that you do!

Something as simple as a hug expresses your love
A precious smile makes it worth my while
A powerful phrase enhances my days
My how I love your ways
Keep spoiling me with simplicity
And I promise that I will always put forth the best in me!

Your Room

Mostly a mess
Rarely clean
Junky computer desk
On the floor, dirty socks and jeans

Your place of refuge
Your private spot
Your secret hiding zone
When you want to be alone

I have a confession to make
Something that I have never told a soul
When you're not around
Your room makes me whole

I go into your room
I think of you and all that you do
I think of the laughs we share and how much we care
I think of the times we fuss and fight and disagree
I remember after all of this you still hug and kiss me

There is nothing but love in this junky room of yours
Remember when you said, "Mommy, I don't know why but it
seems like when I get in your bed, I go right to sleep?",
well, when I lay in your bed, I sleep without a peep

So, even though I fuss about your room being a mess
It serves a much needed purpose
It keeps me going when I am not at my best
It reminds me of what a wonderful blessing you are in my life

I love you!

Just the Way You Are

I love you just the way you are
To me, you are beautiful in every way
I accept you for you
I don't look at you and find reasons to be critical
I look at you and find reasons to love you even more each day
Through you, I find reasons to change myself
Reasons to perfect my imperfections
Each day I learn something from you
Something that will help me to be a better person,
a better friend and a better mother

When you look at your friends, your family, people you may not know and even me, I want you to begin to see the good things in them. Don't be critical, noticing their faults first. Find something good in them and offer encouragement when you see they are not at their best. Offer a helping hand, a kind word or an ear to listen; you may just make someone's day!

We can all learn from someone else and we can all change. I can't change you and you can't change someone else. We all have to make the choice to change ourselves. So, just as I love and accept you the way that you are, I want you to love and accept others just the way they are!

My Only True Love

That you are, without a doubt!
There has never been and never will be one that can cancel you out
A heart of gold
A beautiful face
Nothing and no one can ever take your place

There is nothing like a mother's love
Nothing like the child that holds her love
You, my child, have such an inner peace
A spirit of love,
Oh so sweet

Such beauty and natural grace bestow you
For you, almost anything I would do

I am so proud to call you my love
I thank God each day for such a special gift
Special you are to me, to Him and to all that have
the pleasure of getting in
Into your heart, that perfect place
Lord, I thank you for your unwavering grace

My hero, My love, My joy
You keep me going when it seems there's nowhere to go
You see good when it seems all is bad
You lift up all that is sad
My friend, my child, my girl
There's not another like you in the world!

Voice

You should speak your mind
Of course, there is a right time
There is also a right way
To say what you have to say

You deserve to be heard
I would like to hear your every word

Think before you act and speak
Always use tact
What you say can affect others too
So make sure you wouldn't mind if someone said the same to you

Speak from your heart
Give your words some feeling
Make sure your heart is pure
Otherwise, your words have no meaning

Words with no meaning are words in vain
Words of this nature can cause you shame

God gave you that voice to use
Never use it to be cruel
Always use your voice as a positive tool

Much Love

Much love, that's what I have for you
What a perfect child, all mine too
This is a note just because
Just because, I love you

I think of you each hour of the day
And as the day goes by, my heart always finds something to say
This is what it told me today

Just sharing moments with you fills me with such joy
Through the laughter and the tears, the hugs and the fears
I have realized that there is no one that I
would rather share my years

I have many hopes and dreams for you
My biggest is that I can help you see yours through
Your hopes and dreams mean the world to me
I live my life for God and you, you see

I want you to have all that your heart desires
I want to be by your side when you experience life's fires
I wish to be a friend – a best friend to you
I want to be the best mother too

Thanks again, Lord, the gift from above, I give much love!

Walking Away

Some of my most precious thoughts of you happen when you are walking away. If only you could see the priceless look on my face. At times, I ask myself what could I have possibly done to deserve such a wonderful child. Sometimes, it's "look at her"- I can't believe she's all mine. I even thank God for blessing me with you. I smile with such joy just knowing that with you in my life there will never be a void.

Sometimes, I shake my head and laugh to myself in amazement when I think about how much you've grown and changed from day to day. Each time you walk away, I'm reminded of just how proud I am that you are a part of my life.

This probably sounds silly to you right now, but believe me, when you turn and walk away from me, it's like a constant reminder of just how much you really mean.

Birthday Love

It's your birthday and you're eleven
Wow, I'll bet you are in heaven
You looked so excited yesterday
You said you couldn't wait for today
Well, it's here and I hope it's all you expected
I hope this birthday brings you many blessings
I wish you much joy and happiness
I wish for you laughter and excitement
On this very special day, I wish you the very best
I pray that you will have peace
I pray that your joy is for keeps
I pray that you will pray
And be thankful on this very special day
I am proud that I can be a part of your celebration
I'm thankful that I was granted such an angel
Your birthday is not just exciting for you
It means the world to me too
It means that I was not only able to share another year with you
I've been given the honor of beginning another one too
So, this day is special for both of us
It's your birthday and I want it to be full of love
The gift I give to you is unconditional
It's from the depths of my heart and soul

It's because you help to make me whole
The gift I give to you is precious
It's all my love

Happy Birthday,

Love, Mommy

I Am a Star

God give me the strength to stand on my own
To say no to things that are wrong
Give me a temperament of good cheer
An attitude of courage not fear
Help me to always respect myself so that I can in turn respect others
Lord, most of all, allow me to always see the star
you have made of me

Positive

In order for you to speak positively,
you must first instill it in your mind
Once this is done, an inspiration to others you will find

It has to be at the heart of you, positive to the core
It has to be who you are; negativity you abhor

As I challenge myself, I also challenge you
Stay positive, stay true, stay focused and see it through

Think, talk, and live positively
Unstoppable is what you'll be

Strive to stay this way throughout your life
Believe me, you will live with peace and grace and a lot less strife

Laugh

Every day, find time to play
Say to yourself, "this will be a great day"
Even when it's a heavy load
I promise you, a good laugh will ease the road
Get in a good laugh before the day's end
Don't let the day pass
Without living each moment like it's your very last
Each moment only getting better, better than the rest
Remember to laugh, it always has a way of making your better best!

Be a Kid

You know it's true that God can do all things!

So, in saying that, if He really wanted you to be a grown up, he would not have wasted his time making you a kid first.

I know it seems like you are not growing up fast enough, the older kids seem to have more fun and get to do more things. Your time will come, you'll be able to do those same things soon enough. Right now, you need to focus on being just who you are – a kid!

Believe me, it's not all bad. Believe it or not, it can actually be fun. Enjoy each day, play a lot, laugh a lot, just have a good time. Make some good friends and learn to enjoy them. When you sit back and think, try to think of how you can have more fun. Right now, you should have no worries; someone else does that for you.

Grown-ups have a lot of responsibilities. Take a look around and see all the things that we do. Things like going to work every day, cooking, picking up kids from practice, laundry, cleaning, paying bills, shopping for groceries and so much more. Do you really want this right now? Hmm, grown up or play time... Which is better and which is worse?

Now this is a great opportunity for you to say, "Lord, thank you for making me a kid first!"

Let's Show Some Love

It's so important to love and openly share your love with your children – one day you will see it in action in them. Unfortunately, it seems to be missing in children's lives. More and more children are growing up not hearing the words "I Love you" and not feeling an embrace from a parent, not getting the encouragement and guidance they need to grow up confident and strong and maybe not even having a biological parent in the home. It's unfortunate and in my opinion, it's time to close the gap.

I remember one Memorial Day, my daughter went to visit family and friends. During that visit, everything that she had ever been taught about loving and accepting people for who they are had been violated. One of her relatives, repeatedly degraded a young girl. He called her stupid and made fun of her looks. He constantly verbally attacked her for no apparent reason. Imagine how she felt. The little girl told my daughter that sometimes she cries, other times she just goes to her room and throws things. She said she never talks back; she just takes it. My daughter cried as she told me the story and said that no one should be treated this way. She went on to say she had no desire to ever go back and visit again.

After comforting her and telling her how proud I was of her, I encouraged her to continue to love and be a friend to this child. I told her how important it was for her to start practicing forgiveness and that this experience would only strengthen her and her friend. I went on to say that this child especially needs her love and friend-ship; it might be the only positive she has in her life.

I could not have been more proud of my child. I knew at that moment that she was more than just special, she had so much compassion and I needed to nurture it. That night I wrote the next two pages for my amazing daughter.

Hurt

It hurts you to see her in pain
Its hurts you to feel her shame

You ache all over for her hurt
You cry tears for all it's worth

Your friend is your friend but she has no home
No real home to call her own

No one to hold her when she's alone
No one to warm her when she's cold

Her heart aches for simple pleasures
Her mind explores untouchable treasures

She often wonders about this wonderful life
The one she dreams of every night

Only a child, yet she carries a full load
Not even her fault that she travels this road

You're still optimistic for this blessed child
Hoping and praying all the while
The road will get better
She will get her treasures
She'll even experience the simplest pleasures

Please Lord, allow her dreams to come ten fold
Before a precious heart of gold
Turns to stone

Heart to Heart

It hurt me to see you cry
Tears for your friend
Puddled in your eye

I felt your pain
I cried as you cried
The pain transferred

It makes me proud to know that you can sympathize
With the less fortunate child
A friend that travels a road that you know not how

Encourage your friend, this is what she needs now
Let her know that sunlight follows even the darkest cloud

With a friend like you
She'll make it through
What she's going through now
Will only strengthen the both of you

Keep praying for her
And I'll be praying for you
Hold her close as I do you

Love is a cure
It will help us endure

Heart to Heart
Is where we'll start

Parents, Your Children Are Not You – They Need You!

How many times do our children feel alone or we hear horrible stories about other children who are harming themselves, others or contemplating suicide? It is such a real tragedy and a lot of times we miss the signs even in our own children. There is so much hurt, so much sadness; I want our kids to be happy and to have the confidence to be able to work through their problems, whether it means talking to someone and seeking help or just knowing that it's not that bad and I'll get through!

Oftentimes, I wonder what I can do to help as I encounter children that are struggling. Sometimes, it's hard to know. There are no visible signs and they don't open up and tell you that there is something wrong. This is a tough one and it plagues so many young people. How do we get in? I wonder that one too.

We need to find a way in. Our youth need us to be present, persistent, open to their hurts and to listen. It's hard, I know, we have to sometimes open our eyes, quiet our minds and hush our thoughts so we can truly see and hear them. We have to stop saying and thinking that it can't be my child or my child wouldn't do that. We miss it at times because we are so quick to interject our thoughts and our wishes for them and what we think they need to do. Now, granted, we do have some experience, just remember our experiences and lessons were for us and theirs are for them. They are individuals and they internalize and respond to challenge, loss and difficulties in life in their own individual way. As adults, it is important to let them express themselves and teach them how to respond. One way of teaching comes through listening, asking questions and guiding not telling them everything they need to do and how they need to go about doing it. When I say listening, I mean truly listening. Stop listening and thinking about what you are going to say at the same time because you really aren't listening! Stop cutting them off and shutting them up – allow them to speak and express themselves. Our children need to be heard; sometimes, the message is not in what they say but how it is said and the feeling behind it. How will you catch it if you only hear a part of what they are saying because you have your own agenda.

Sometimes, it is about just guiding and nudging them and letting them come up with the solutions knowing they have our support. We have to help them develop those problem solving skills at a young age so they are able to easily navigate challenge when it arises.

Opening the door to fluid conversation, not judgment will help. We don't always look at it as judgment when it's our child. Think about your child or yourself for that matter. How would it feel being told you did it wrong and you should have done this, that or the other? Would it be better if someone helped you to build confidence by asking you what you think you should have done and then complimented you when you come up with a good solution? Our kids deserve that from us. This is a skill that will serve them throughout life.

How many times have you said to your child, "when I was your age, I..." Expecting our kids to be like us is a mistake. They are sooooo themselves and that is perfectly fine! They have their own identity and we should be encouraging them to be who they are and nurturing their growth as they come into their own. You might say you don't expect them to be like you and you respect their individuality, but ask yourself why you get so disappointed or mad when they don't like the things you think they should like. Or, when they say they want to be an actor instead of a Doctor. What about when they want to go into the Peace Corp instead of going to college and getting what we call a "good job." It's hard, I experienced it. Something as simple as shopping; I wanted my daughter to want to go shopping with me because I liked it. She didn't want to go shopping ever and it was a mystery to me, she was a teenager and every teenage girl liked shopping. I wanted her to run track because I did it, she tried it and was very good at it but when she said she didn't like it, I was disappointed and assumed it was because she was a little bit lazy. She liked to read a lot and wanted to play in the band. Well, I was totally different at her age. That was me and I had to realize that her path was for her and her likes being different from mine didn't make her any less of a person or a disappointment, it was who she was and that was by design. I learned to nurture her; I encouraged her to follow her dreams and to be passionate. Luckily, I was able to redirect my thoughts and actions before I destroyed her confidence in herself. She wanted so much to please me even at the expense of her own unhappiness. I started to see a glimpse of insecurity in her. I didn't want my child to be unhappy; I wanted her to flourish.

Think about it, encourage your child to be ok with themselves. Ask them what they like and let them know that it is ok to be different. Make sure they know that you want them to be happy and you will support them even if their likes don't align with what you want for them. Let them know that you want the best for them and the best is letting them grow in their own identity. Their gifts and talents are theirs and you want to see them in full bloom. Nurture their passions and don't expect them to be like you or have the same likes, dreams and passions as you. They will make mistakes; help them to grow from them and teach them how to deal with challenge, pain and change.

Superstar

Superstar athlete I'm not
No desire to bounce a ball or
Make a shot

Can't run fast
Or catch a touchdown pass
This doesn't make me any less of a man
My dreams are real
And I deserve a chance

Judging me
Calling me names
Just because I don't play your game

Because it's right for you
Doesn't make it right for me
I refuse to settle
I won't pretend
I will never give in

God gave us all our own special gifts
Our own talents
To use for his will

So, athlete, I'm not
Superstar, meant to be!

Young Destruction

What is this you say?
"I don't love myself"
"There's nothing good about me"
"Nobody loves me, not even my mother"
"I don't go to school, 'cause I don't like it and it don't like me!"
"Maybe if I kill myself, I won't have to hurt anymore"
"I'm 16 and not even in high school"
"My life will never change"

Child, what are you doing to yourself?
What could possibly make you think these awful things?
What happened to your love?
Who took it from you?
Who robbed you of your joy?
Who stole what was yours and only yours?
Why did your heart turn cold?
When it was given, it was a heart of pure gold

Why can't you love yourself?
You will never be able to love anyone else
Don't you care?
Don't you even care?
What will become of you?

How can I help?
What can I do?
Let me help you get it back?
I want to see you get through

I care, I care even when you don't
I'm there when it seems no one else is
I'll be your legs, when it seems you can't walk
I'll carry the load when your back gives out
Talk to me, just talk to me
Trust me
I have faith in you
I believe in you
Child, I love you

I Love You, No Matter What

No matter the problem
How deep the rut
I love you
Even when you don't like me
Or know how to trust
I still love you
Your hurts and your struggles
Push me to spend more time focusing on you
I see you
I see you
I really do
I see your actions
I see your heart
I see your dreams even though to you they seem afar
I listen to your words
I hear your worries, your fears
I feel you
Your pain seeps through your mask
Gushing across your cheeks
I'm here for you
I'll talk to you
I'll listen too
I'll slow down and make time just for you

I'll encourage you and show you the way
I love you
If patience is what you need
Patient is what I'll be
You are so precious to me
Your gifts deserve to be unleashed
I envision you healed
I see it
You're already whole
I see what you've become
You know the treasure you hold
I'm proud of you
You learned to live and you love your life !

Girl, Get Up!

How many times do we defeat ourselves by our thoughts and our response to challenges? Life is our friend, ladies! That's an odd way of looking at it, I know, but if you think about it, how powerful are we that we can overcome our challenges and stand stronger after each one? I look back at the many obstacles and all of the things that I have been bothered by throughout my life and my, oh my, I am still here! And not just here; I am much stronger, happier and better. Best of all, I have something to share with you to hopefully inspire you to always move forward.

I have truly changed my mindset about stress, fear and life's difficulties. I am embracing every challenge as my opportunity to stand in confidence knowing that when I succeed, eventually, someone else will benefit. I will have another success story to possibly help someone shake off whatever it is that's keeping them from being their best.

So, get up, reach deep within, it's in there, I promise you! Pull out your power, your passion, your conquerer attitude and stand tall in confidence. When you feel bogged down or discouraged, know that your power is stronger than any imaginary weight. I know life's problems are real and I am not making light of it; I just know from experience that it is how we respond to our fears and problems that determines our outcome.

Find the music that makes your heart, soul, mind and body dance. Play it, put it on repeat and DANCE! Every day, when waking up and engaging life, whether it is work, relationships, vacation, community service, etc...dance through it. Find your music, your passion and live like a dancing machine. Sometimes, you have to change your dance depending on the song, speed it up, slow it down, wobble, electric slide or maybe even a two step. I am convinced that life will start to look and feel better and your response to everyday challenge and facing your fears will be different.

Remember, life is your friend. Sometimes, it is very hard to see our way out of life's mess. I mean when the tidal waves hit, it's hard to weather the storm. It's all about how we choose to respond and my response is to put my dancing shoes on and dance my way out or at least to a better situation.

My experiences were not easy to deal with and I did not always respond quickly with the right choice. Sometimes, I ran or blamed others for my storm. Well, as you can imagine, that didn't help and the issues went nowhere. When I was finally ready to dance, I had to look in that mirror again and see me! I had to be honest with myself and deal with myself and all of those things that perpetuated my issues. My problems did not come because someone did something to me, they weren't prolonged because someone stood in the way; I was in my own way the majority of the time.

My call out to you: Girl, Get Up! Be bold, be your beautiful, powerful and confident self and get out of your way! Look your fears and insecurities right in the face and dance until they are no longer taking up space on your dance floor!

Pain

What is it about me that makes me susceptible to pain?
I wish I knew so I could make a change
Why is my name followed by gloom?
I never see the sun, only the moon

How did I become acquainted with the dark shadow?
Murkiness raining down
Dim clouds lurking around
Fogginess on the prowl

How long do I travel this one-way street?
Is there a detour that ends the grief?
How long is this desolate journey?
How long do I continue to step on my own feet?

I can't call you friend, yet you share my deepest thoughts
My most guarded secrets are yours to keep
Not a companion, still you invade my dreams
Plaguing my sleep as if you were meant to be

How do I bypass this sorrow stricken trail?
I wasn't created to live in hell
It's not for me, I was meant to prevail

I refuse to live in anguish
Misery cannot inhabit me
I am triumphant over what's ailing me!

Find your Beauty

Find your inner joy
You've hidden your beauty
Somewhere in a shell
Find it for yourself
It's time to take it off the shelf
Put it on, wear it
So you can parade in your peace
Look deep, look high and low
Find it
Find it so you can grow
See it
See your beauty as it is
Don't be afraid to put it on
Step into it, it's yours
It's there
Bask in it
Relax and take it all in
Love it
Take pride in your beauty, be bold
It was given only to you, it's yours to behold
I can see it
I can feel it
I am often amazed by it when in your presence

Find your peace
Your beauty
Your happiness
It's there
Somewhere on a shelf
Waiting for you to start loving yourself

Inside Grind

There is so much more to this struggle than what you can see
It's a struggle for peace, pride and serenity
A war of emotions clouding your view
A longing for love that entraps you
This battle is not yours
You've heard this before
Give it to Him
Surrender and let Him win
Your peace is just within reach
Don't be afraid to open up
Let Him show up
Open your eyes and your mind
See what comfort arises from this grind
There's comfort in it
There's peace in it
It is yours
It was yours from the very beginning
Long for the love of the one who can strip your pride
The one that can instill true love inside
The one that can heal all hurt
The one that has sealed your total worth
Right now I cry for you
Because you have not received your due

But I smile too
Because I know your due is due you

My Wish for You

I wish your pain away
For you, I wish a brighter day
I wish a never ending peace
For you, I wish no more thorns at your feet
I wish for you serenity in your life
For you, I wish freedom from strife
I wish for you tranquility
At first glimpse of pain's sting
For you, I wish stillness, no more hurt lingering
No more grimace or scowl
For you, I wish that used to be smile
I wish calmness and quietude
I wish a joyful interlude
For you, I wish a break from the struggle
A rest from any sign of trouble
For no one is more deserving of this wish than you
Now, I shall pray to the most high
That it all comes true

Troublesome Times

You are experiencing some troublesome times
Surely, they will only last for a while
Your troubles will soon be over
And you can marvel at your victory
Remind yourself that you are triumphant during conflict
Weariness cannot rest on your shoulders
Only bothersome for a season
You're a warrior
One who battles to succeed
Put on your armor
Seize your peace
You're not alone, I'm with you
Together we'll achieve
In troublesome times
There's character building
Faith strengthening
Mind purifying
Heart cleansing
This is ours for the taking
New armor in the making
So, don't let trouble get the best of you
It can only be bothersome for its due

Loneliness,
this is Not Your Home!

I made some choices in my life now I feel so alone
Where do I go with this? I feel so alone
I am so strong but I am still alone
I am tired of being strong
I want more
I want a shoulder to lean on
I don't want to be alone
This feeling is not productive
It brings me down
I have to hide it and keep my smile on
Deep inside, I cringe
I hurt and I hurt – I am so alone
I want help but no one understands
I haven't told a soul
No one can know
I want to talk but no one seems right
How do I get this out? I need to fight
This feeling of loneliness
This hurt and sadness
I need for someone to hear my heart
And speak peace

It's trying to break me, keep me from being my best
It wakes me at night, breaking my rest
I don't like being by myself because I have to face me
I have to face this loneliness which frightens me
I want more, I deserve more
I want to walk in my boldness
I want to own me and be free
I want to be who I know I was created to be

Girl, get up! Walk with me
Let me show you what a true friend can be
I love you and want you to be free
You don't have to worry
I am your friend
Dig deep within, your true identity you'll see
Loneliness is not you, it was never meant to be
Your choices in life made you better and stronger
Loneliness cannot live in your space any longer!

Not You

He was clear about not wanting you
You refused to see
He said nothing, but showed it all
You refused to listen to the noise

He didn't have to ask to see you
You asked him to come
He didn't have to call
You called him

He didn't have to miss you
He never responded when you said you missed him
You wanted daylight
He gave you only nights

He never had to try
He didn't want to try
He knew early on it was not you
He stayed because you asked him to

It was easy
It was convenient
It was real
As real as your imagination

Woman, why are you sad?
Let him be
Erase your hurt
Know your worth
He was not yours from the beginning
It was obvious it was not you
Listen and wait for your queue
Let yours come to you
You are worth the chase
Be patient, you are also worth the wait!

Own Your Worth!

Ladies, why short change yourself
You deserve the absolute best
Treat yourself well
And demand the utmost respect
Know your worth
Show your worth
Live your worth
Own your worth

Accept only that which can add to you
Only those who can complement you
Invite only the one who appreciates your worth
Those who will encourage and celebrate your growth

Does his presence rob you of your dance?
Does it make you wish you hadn't taken a chance?
Does it strip you of your pride?
Girl, he is not worth your time

Only include him if he is the melody that makes you dance
He has to be worthy of your choice
He has to love himself and know his own worth

Is he worthy of your presence?
He said he chose you
He only pursued you
His chase didn't change your name
You had a choice to make

Ladies, it's time to choose you
Invest in your own happiness
Wake up and see it for what it is
Acknowledge your worth
Let nothing get in the way of your progress
Accept only that which compliments you and your best

Just Talk to Him

Do you ever think about praying but don't know exactly what to say? When I sat down and thought about praying two things came to my mind; acknowledgement and thanks. I know I need to acknowledge the presence of God and thank Him for being everything to me. At times, I feel the need to talk to God just to talk and that's ok.

Some say pray, I say God let's talk. Sometimes, I do all the talking because I just want him to know how much I appreciate and love Him. Sometimes, I talk and then I just listen – that's when I really need to hear from Him.

Here are a couple of prayers I wrote just because I wanted to talk to God!

Lord, I Love You

Lord, I love you for being you
I trust you to guide me and see me through
I give you all the praise because you are more than worthy
I fear you because you are all mighty
Lord, I bless you, because you have truly blessed me
All that I am, Lord, is because of you
I treasure your word because I know it's true
Lord, you are more than a father, you're everything to me
You're the path that I walk
The language that I talk
You're every single strand of hair that grows on my head
You're the hand that rubs my back and tucks me into bed
You're the voice that awakens me from a deep sleep
You're the special peace that I keep
You're the calmness that takes over when the tide is high
You're that sweet breath of fragrant air that wipes all my tears dry
Lord, I adore you
I worship you
And most of all, Lord, I Love You!

Thank you Lord

Thank you, Lord, for creating me
Thank you for showing me that there's no limit to what I can be
Thank you, Lord, for being my family when it seems
my family's not near
Thank you for being my strength,
for holding me close and for loving me most
Thank you for my friends and my enemies
Through them I have learned love and forgiveness
Thank you, Lord, for giving me peace
when a storm was brewing amidst
Lord, I thank you for the poor and less fortunate
Because of them I have learned grace and humility
Thank you for the wrong turns
I now seek you for direction
I thank you, Lord, for teaching me to pray
Through prayer I can always talk to you
And thank you Lord for just being you
Because without you, none of this would be true!

My Dad

I cannot complete this without sharing a little about my father – this would not be possible if he were not a part of my life. He was an awesome man and I miss him dearly. We all experience loss at some point in our lives and it is never easy. My dad instilled so much in me, he was such a gentle, kind and honorable man; he was loving, truly role modeled strength, courage and wisdom.

My dad was a father to his biological children but stood in the gap for many others. He nurtured in his own way which continuously blessed others. I am so grateful to have had a father in my life who loved and cared about his family. You know, at times, I find myself thinking about him when I experience challenges and that thought alone pushes me to move forward.

I wrote this for my family when my dad transitioned from this life and I share with you because I hope that as you experience loss in your journey, it will provide you with comfort.

Your Angel

I've pressed on beyond the wind and the trees
Far beyond this season
Oh yes, God had a reason
I'm needed in a much greater way
I know it's hard to understand
Just remember, life as you know it
is only the beginning of the eternal plan
Trust in HIM
Partner with your faith
Become one
Know that HE makes no mistakes
I soar with you each day
When you rise, I rise
When you breathe, I breathe
Exhale and release your sadness
Inhale and feel my presence
It's impossible to leave you
We have been one from the start, we share a heart
I am in your thoughts
I'm in your prayers
I'm in your everyday talk
There is no void, no empty hole
I'm always there

You've got my soul
Smile when you think of me
Laughter shall fill your heart
Enjoy all of life's trinkets
Embrace my transition
I am still God's gift

You haven't lost a husband or friend
Parent or grandparent
Son or daughter
Brother or sister
Aunt or uncle
You've gained inspiration
You've learned to treasure the smallest of things
You've learned to love now, not in a minute
Forgiveness is in your heart
Love is on your tongue
Peace is on the way
For an Angel you've gained today!

A Little Bit of Honey to Sweeten the Pot!

Find the music that makes your heart, soul, mind and body dance. Play it, put it on repeat and DANCE!

Look deep within, pull out your power, your confidence, and your strength. Never doubt that you are worth it or worthy; Girl, You Deserve it!

GIRLY – Tell yourself every single day "Girl, I really love you" and mean it with all of your heart! Then make a point to tell someone else.

It's ok to tell yourself and feel that you are beautiful because you absolutely are!

Each of us was created differently on purpose; love and accept each other for who they are not who you think or want them to be – this includes our children.

Plans get messed up on purpose because they do not fit your true purpose.

Embrace love, share love, speak love and spark love!

Girl, Get Up! Be bold, be your beautiful, powerful and confident self and get out of your way!

Give of yourself – learn to be a friend, a shoulder, a support system, an encourager, an inspiration and a role model.

Life truly is your friend! Embrace it and everything that it has for you...learn to love it as you live it.

CHARM – commit to Change Hearts as a Role Model every day.

Look in your mirror as often as you can and love what you see.

You are bigger and more powerful than your fears...Push through your fears and love what it propels you to achieve!

Worthy, you are so Worthy! Encourage yourself; you are worth it, you deserve it! It will be hard to encourage someone else if you struggle encouraging yourself.

Your voice can be a life changer! Use it to inspire life, grace, love, peace and freedom.

Make time to be grateful and acknowledge God for his grace and blessings. Make time to talk to God, some call it prayer!

A Moment for Me

I encourage you to take a moment each day and look in the mirror and say something nice to yourself. It doesn't matter what it is; it is between you and your mirror. Feeling good about ourselves shows up in so many ways. This is about establishing confidence in who you are and accepting yourself just the way you are – we all have areas where we might want to improve; let's learn to be ok with who we are first. Here are some things I say to myself; sometimes, I am not in the mirror:

- I love me some me just the way I am

- I am blessed

- I have a great smile

- I am special, I am beautiful and I am proud of myself

- I am confident and I look fine

- I am a good friend

- I am a winner

- I am smart

- I trust myself

- I make mistakes, I admit them, I learn and move on

- I am honest

- I am kind
- My feet are fine (not the prettiest, but they are fine)
- My skin is just right and my nose is perfect
- I can and I will succeed
- I forgive myself and I forgive others quickly
- I am loved by so many people
- I know how to love

About the Author

Angela Sweetenberg grew up in Roanoke, Virginia, and received her Bachelor's Degree in Business Administration Management and a Master's Degree in Management and Leadership from Liberty University. Angela has many years of leadership experience and is currently serving as a leader within her organization and is a Certified Professional Coach through World Coach Institute.

Angela is passionate about personal and professional growth; she loves coaching and mentoring others. Bold, courageous, relentless, driven, passionate and purposeful are all words that describe Angela. Her goal is to inspire confidence and build a strong network of confident women and girls. Angela spends much of her spare time with friends and family and nurturing her hobby, writing. Publishing some of her work has been an aspiration for many years.

Angela has a beautiful daughter, Briona, who is the inspiration for many of the writings in this book. She loves her large family including her foster daughter, Stephany, two brothers, two sisters, sisters in law, nieces, nephews, cousins, aunts and uncles. Angela gives a special tribute to her mother, Georgia Sweetenberg, who has been a rock in her life! Also, her Kingdom Life Ministries, Intl. family who has been a great support system and teacher of all things "LOVE".

Angela is available for conferences, seminars and as a guest speaker. Please contact her at angelaswe1@gmail.com.

www.ingramcontent.com/pod-product-compliance
Lightning Source LLC
Chambersburg PA
CBHW062000040426
42447CB00010B/1831